# How to use the stickers

First find what you've got to look out for under this sign **Lookout!** Then peel off a sticker with the right number of points and stick it in the blank circle.

Score 20 for Hampton Court Palace where Henry lived

Score 20 for Windsor Castle where Henry is buried

Score 10 for Henry VIII's coat-of-arms on castles and palaces

Score 15 for an abbot's house in a monastery

Score 15 for treasures from churches

Score 10 for a ruin of a monastery

Score 10 for a big house built in Tudor times

Answer: page 14 A star

# Who was 'Enry?

**H**enry VIII was King of England from 1509 until 1547. He had six wives. His first wife was Catherine of Aragon.

**H**enry and Catherine were married for twenty four years. They had six children but only one girl survived. Henry wanted a son to rule after him. Catherine had become too old to have any more children. So in 1533 he decided to divorce Catherine and marry Anne Boleyn. Henry hoped Anne would give him a son.

What was the first thing Henry did when he came to the throne?

He sat down!

## Lookout!

Look out for Hampton Court Palace where Henry lived and Windsor Castle where he is buried. Find out what you score on page 2.

Henry was very powerful. But the Church was mighty too. Bishops and archbishops helped to run the country. The Church owned about a third of all the land in England, ran schools and hospitals, looked after travellers and helped the poor.

*The tomb of Catherine of Aragon in Peterborough Cathedral.*

# A huge row

When Henry became King, everyone in England was a Catholic. The Catholic Church was ruled by the Pope who lived in Rome, Italy.

Henry had to get permission from the Pope to divorce Catherine. The Pope refused to give him a divorce, so Henry decided to break away from the Catholic Church. He made himself Head of the Church of England. This meant he didn't have to ask the Pope's permission to do anything.

**Lookout!**

Look out for Henry VIII's coat-of-arms on castles and palaces. Find out what you score on page 2.

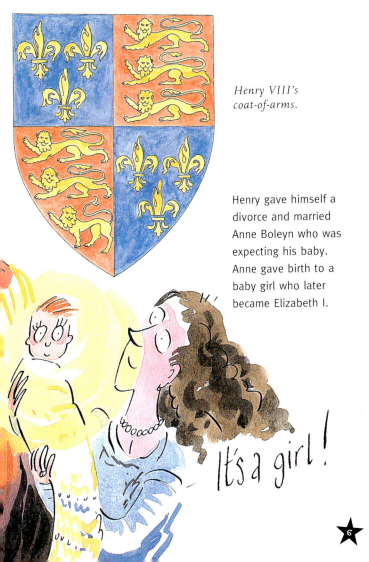

*Henry VIII's coat-of-arms.*

Henry gave himself a divorce and married Anne Boleyn who was expecting his baby. Anne gave birth to a baby girl who later became Elizabeth I.

It's a girl!

# More power for 'Enry

**H**enry was now extra powerful. But he needed money for the wars he was fighting in France. How could he get some more money?

**D**uring the Middle Ages the Church had become very rich. Henry cast a beady eye over all the land and treasures that monasteries owned. Then he had a cunning plan. He would close all the monasteries and take all their land and riches for himself! But he needed a good excuse.

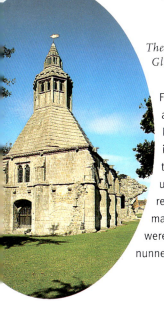

*The Abbot's kitchen at Glastonbury Abbey.*

First he had to prove that monks and nuns no longer led a holy life. It was true that many people living in monasteries enjoyed the very things they were supposed to give up. Some took holidays, most had regular wages and some even got married. Abbots and abbesses who were in charge of monasteries and nunneries often lived in great luxury.

Henry decided to close all the monasteries down by force.

## Lookout!

Look out for the ruins of an abbot's house in a monastery. Find out what you score on page 2.

8

# Thomas Cromwell

Thomas Cromwell was Henry's chief minister. **Henry put Thomas in charge of closing the monasteries down.**

Thomas's first job was to find out how much all the monasteries and nunneries were worth. All land, buildings and treasures owned by the Church had to be valued. His second job was to find out which monasteries were well known for bad behaviour.

*A chalice, part of the treasure owned by a monastery.*

**Lookout!**

Look out for treasures from churches in museums and cathedral treasuries. Find out what you score on page 2.

# When you get home . . .

. . . make this DECORATED CANDLE.
You will need a white candle, gold paint,
a paper doily, masking tape, a stencil
brush. Cut off a bit of the doily. Fasten
it to the candle with tape. Stencil through

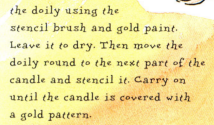

the doily using the
stencil brush and gold paint.
Leave it to dry. Then move the
doily round to the next part of the
candle and stencil it. Carry on
until the candle is covered with
a gold pattern.

In 1536 Thomas
ordered that all
poor monasteries
with less than
twelve monks had
to close. Then,
three years later,
all other
monasteries had
to close.

CROSSES(gold)
CROSSES(jewelled)
CANDLESTICKS

# The damage

When Henry became King there were about 800 monasteries in England. When he died there were none.

Thomas and his men set about destroying all monasteries. They smashed tombs, windows and statues. Jewels and treasures were carted off. Monastery buildings were pulled down and the land sold off. Floorboards, furniture and paintings were burnt, roofs were stripped of lead and bells were melted down.

*The ruins of Fountains Abbey in Yorkshire.*

**Lookout!**

Look out for ruins of monasteries. Find out what you score on page 2.

Thousands of monks and nuns were given money and sent away. Abbots and abbesses who co-operated with Thomas were given big houses and a lot of money. Those who didn't were executed.

# What happened next?

Closing down the monasteries brought about some of the biggest changes England has ever known.

Some monks and nuns got jobs in churches outside monasteries. Others fled abroad to start a new life. Some got married. In some towns, people saved the monastery church by raising the money and buying it from Henry.

TUDOR REMOVALS